TOM PIERRE

How to Gain Weight with a Fast Metabolism?

Contents

Chapter 1 - The Struggle of Gaining Weight	1
Chapter 2 - Today's Society Don't Promote Healthy Weight...	8
Chapter 3 - Before Starting your Weight Gain Journey, FIX...	15
Chapter 4 - 3 Rules to Master for Gaining Weight	30
Chapter 5 - Best Foods to Gain Weight	36
Chapter 6 - Weight Gain Meal Plan for 1 Week	49
Chapter 7 - Common mistakes	53
Chapter 8 - Best Supplements to Support Weight Gain	58
Chapter 9 - Sport and Activity to Gain Weight	71
Chapter 10 - Delicious Weight Gain Recipes	78
Chapter 11 - Tips for Staying Motivated	99
Chapter 12 - How to Increase Calories Without Changing...	103
Conclusion	107
Resources	108

Chapter 1 - The Struggle of Gaining Weight

When you're naturally skinny, gaining weight can be challenging or even extremely difficult. Our metabolism is so fast that we burn an enormous amount of energy each day, often more than we consume. That's why the numbers on the scale don't increase.

A person with a fast metabolism will burn much more energy than someone with a normal metabolism. This is an advantage from a health and aesthetic perspective because we store less fat than the average person. However, on the flip side, we have a hard time gaining weight, whether it's muscle for men, a bit of fat, or feminine curves for women.

But with the right strategy, you can gain weight gradually while maintaining your health. I emphasize this point because many people, myself included, have compromised their health, particularly their gut health, by trying to gain weight at any cost. Yet gut health is the cornerstone of weight gain and overall health.

Before attempting to gain weight when you're naturally skinny, it's crucial to understand what you're doing. I'm going to share my story and how it took me over six years to gain weight and understand the mechanism of weight gain for those with a fast metabolism. As you'll see, my journey was filled with obstacles, and many times, I yo-yoed back to my initial weight.

At 18, I weighed 108 pounds at 5'10".

CHAPTER 1 - THE STRUGGLE OF GAINING WEIGHT

8 September 2019 at 12:56

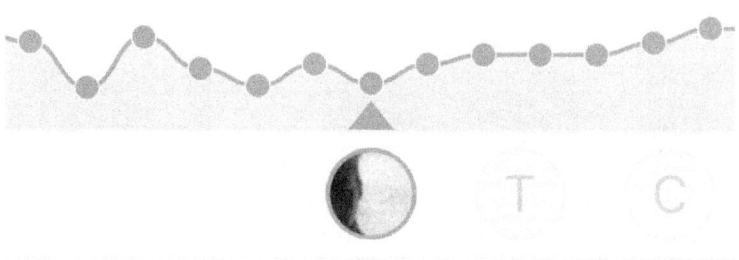

I had an extremely fast metabolism and had eaten small portions all my life. At 18, I clearly had the body of a 12-year-old child. I felt disconnected from my self-image and my body. I love cinema and have seen actors like Daniel Craig (in James

Bond), Ryan Gosling, and Paul Newman, who had athletic and masculine physiques… and it made me dream. Even having a "normal" weight without being muscular was a dream for me.

I had just started university and wanted to gain weight quickly. So I began stuffing myself with milk, bananas, oatmeal, and peanut butter smoothies. I also ate red beans with rice daily because red beans were considered a good source of protein. I ate a lot of lentils with spaghetti too. Veganism was very trendy at that time, and it had a negative influence on me even though I wasn't vegan. I also ate a lot of chicken and some ground beef occasionally.

The problem is that I unknowingly jeopardized my gut health progressively. You have to be extremely careful because once gut health is compromised, it impacts your overall health. Don't make the same mistake. After several months on this diet, I started developing acne (which I had never had except on my back) because my nutrition was poor. Indeed, stuffing yourself with lentils and red beans, full of fiber and anti-nutrients, **disrupts the gut microbiome and intestinal lining**.

It's a vicious cycle because once gut health is compromised, you absorb less of what you eat. So it has the opposite effect on weight gain because you absorb less energy. It's very, very bad.

I also developed lactose intolerance, which I didn't have at all when my diet was more balanced and less drastic. This worsened my acne, but I still gorged on peanut butter, a massive source of unsaturated fat that oxidizes in the body and creates oxidative stress.

CHAPTER 1 - THE STRUGGLE OF GAINING WEIGHT

So when I decided to gain weight in the beginning, I unnecessarily stressed my body and disrupted my microbiome, which significantly slowed down my weight gain journey. My intestinal barrier took a hit and was no longer as strong as before.

Maybe a year after I started, I went to the Canary Islands and ate some fish that wasn't very fresh. Since my immune system had weakened due to my unbalanced nutrition, I immediately got **food poisoning**, which further slowed my weight gain. It took me months to recover, with abdominal pain and heartburn every time I stressed my stomach, either by eating or exercising. The body takes months and months to recover from this kind of infection.

But at that time, I was interested in nutrition from a distant perspective without necessarily digging deeper, and I followed the recommendations of YouTubers or influencers in the fitness field for muscle gain. The advice was simple: eat oatmeal, banana/peanut butter smoothies, rice with chicken and broccoli. All of this in large quantities, and you'll gain weight. **Often, the people giving this advice aren't naturally skinny with a fast metabolism themselves.**

Since then, I've become interested in nutrition and how the human body is working holistically. I've also explored supplementation, vitamins, minerals, and medicinal herbs. I went through a phase where **I had dozens of supplements to take each day**... I also became extremely interested in gut health because I had many problems in this area due to an unbalanced diet.

And by studying all these things, I found strategies to gain weight. It's only by taking a deep interest in something that you understand the field. And you need a very global approach to understand all the ins and outs. It's not enough to focus on weight gain; you need to understand how the body functions and energy storage in particular.

I started at 108 pounds, and **now I weigh over 143 pound**s. I still have a few pounds to gain, but I know I'll get there gradually. There are small strategies that have brought me enormous results. Whereas before, I had a drastic nutrition plan, and it didn't bring me much results.

In this book, I'm going to share what worked for me and what should work for you. Remember, I weighed 108 pounds! Imagine an 18-year-old guy weighing 108 pounds at 5'10". Today I feel much better in my skin, and despite this weight gain, my body is almost as athletic as before. Yes, it is possible to gain weight without necessarily gaining fat. But that shouldn't scare you because, with a fast metabolism, we generally store very little fat.

As a small anecdote, I now have enough fat to float in the water in a starfish position and enjoy this sensation in the Mediterranean Sea. I had never understood why I couldn't float in this position, and it was simply because I didn't have enough fat. I was exactly at 5% body fat. To give you an idea, bodybuilders use steroids and medications before competitions to try to burn fat and reach 5% on the day of the show. Today, I'm around 10-15%, and I feel much better in my skin: muscles, energy, libido, body temperature...

Because you'll see during your weight gain, **all your signs of vitality will improve**. This is true for both men and women.

I hope this story has inspired you and will motivate you to apply the strategies I'm going to give you in this book. Above all, try to apply the advice in this book gradually. If your gut health isn't optimal, if you're often constipated, for example, try to implement the advice on this point first before changing everything directly. Apply one thing and see if it's positive for you.

Now let's see why today's world isn't ideal to gain **healthy** weight and how to fix it.

Chapter 2 - Today's Society Don't Promote Healthy Weight Gain

In our modern world, gaining healthy weight has become surprisingly challenging. While obesity rates continue to rise, those who struggle to put on weight often find themselves swimming against the current societal norms.

Processed food: Calorie-dense but nutrient-poor foods are counterproductive

One might think that the abundance of high-calorie foods in our society would make weight gain easier. However, the reality is quite different. Junk food, while calorie-dense, is often nutrient-poor. This creates a paradoxical situation where you can consume a lot of calories without providing your body the necessary building blocks for healthy weight gain.

Fast food and packaged snacks may seem like an easy way to increase calorie intake, but they often lead to inflammation, gut health issues, and metabolic problems. These foods can actually hinder your body's ability to gain weight effectively, as they don't support muscle growth or overall health. I remember eating instant noodles after school because it was easy and quick to make… yet it is one of the worst processed foods you can eat.

Instead of relying on processed, **focus on nutrient-dense whole foods that provide not just calories, but also the vitamins, minerals, and other nutrients your body needs to gain weight and maintain health**. Opt for foods like eggs, grass-fed meats, honey, and milk (A2 or goat milk if you have already some lactose reactions)… more on this later. These options will support your weight gain goals while also promoting overall health.

Problematic smoothies: issues with typical "weight gain" smoothies

Many weight gain programs recommend high-calorie smoothies, often consisting of ingredients like bananas, milk, oatmeal, and peanut butter.

HOW TO GAIN WEIGHT WITH A FAST METABOLISM?

While these smoothies can indeed be calorie-dense, they come with several issues:

1. **Digestive stress**: Combining multiple food groups (fruits, grains, and nuts) in one meal can be difficult for some people to digest, especially those with sensitive stomachs. Even if your stomach isn't sensible today: eat this daily and you will feel your stomach become more and more sensitive...
2. **Blood sugar spikes:** The combination of high-sugar fruits and quick-digesting carbs can lead to rapid blood sugar increases, followed by crashes that may affect energy levels

and appetite.
3. **Potential allergens:** Many people have sensitivities to common smoothie ingredients like milk or peanuts, which can cause inflammation and hinder weight gain efforts. What's more, peanuts are full of anti-nutrients and partially "block" the nutrients of the smoothie.
4. **Weak digestive power:** I used to drink this smoothie around 4 pm as a snack. But to digest, the body needs to feel that you're chewing, so digestion is much more efficient. This is not the case with a smoothie that you drink.

Instead of relying on these problematic smoothies, consider alternatives that are easier to digest and more balanced in nutrients. We will see further in this book.

Stressful environment: Impact of modern stress on metabolism and appetite

Our fast-paced, always-connected lifestyle has led to unprecedented levels of chronic stress. This constant state of *"fight or flight"* can have a significant impact on our ability to gain weight. Stress hormones like cortisol can increase metabolism, making it harder to put on weight. Additionally, stress can suppress appetite in some individuals, further complicating weight gain efforts.

To counteract this, it's crucial to incorporate stress-reduction techniques into your daily routine. This might include practices like meditation, deep breathing exercises, or simply setting aside time for relaxation and hobbies.

Personally, I like to do a **vagus nerve reset** before sleeping and sometimes before eating. It takes 1 minute and immediately relaxes you. You'll find the video tutorial about this technique on the resource page (check the QR code at the end of the book).

By managing stress, you create a more favorable internal environment for healthy weight gain.

Importance of eating in a calm environment

I used to make a mistake when I started to live in my university flat: eating while watching a video. Yet, the environment in which we eat plays a crucial role in our digestion and nutrient absorption.

Yes, eating on the go, while watching a video, while working, or in a stressful environment can negatively impact our body's ability to process food effectively. When we're stressed or distracted, our body diverts energy away from digestion, potentially leading to poor nutrient absorption and digestive issues.

Make an effort to **create a calm, relaxed environment for your meals**. The best is to eat with other people. But if you're alone, make an effort and turn off screens, sit down at a table, and take time to enjoy your food. At first, it is hard but after a few days, it becomes normal.

This mindful approach to eating can improve digestion, increase enjoyment of meals, and potentially help you consume more calories without feeling overly full.

Nutrient density affected by soil quality and over-processed foods

The quality of our food has been declining over the decades due to several factors. "Modern" agricultural practices have led to soil depletion, resulting in produce that is less nutrient-dense than it was in the past. Additionally, the rise of ultra-processed foods means that a significant portion of many people's diets comes from products that are far removed from their natural state.

This decrease in "real food" consumption makes it harder to gain weight healthily. Even if you're eating enough calories, **you might not be getting the micronutrients necessary for optimal health and weight gain**.

To combat this, prioritize whole, minimally processed foods in your diet. Choose organic produce when possible, as it tends to be grown in healthier soil. One effective way to access higher quality, more nutrient-dense food is to shop at local farmer's markets.

Produce at farmer's markets is often harvested within a day or two of being sold, meaning it retains more nutrients than food that has traveled long distances and sat on supermarket shelves. You will also eat more seasonally. Eating seasonally ensures a natural variety in your diet and often means consuming produce at its peak nutritional value. Small, local farmers often use more sustainable farming practices that maintain soil health, resulting in more nutrient-dense produce.

By incorporating farmer's market shopping into your routine, you can **access higher quality products** that will support your weight gain goals more effectively than conventionally grown supermarket options. We will see what are the best foods to get at the farmer's market later. And if you don't have the budget for it, we'll see some alternatives.

Chapter 3 - Before Starting your Weight Gain Journey, FIX this

Before embarking on your weight gain journey, it's crucial to address some fundamental aspects of your health. These foundational elements will not only support your weight gain efforts but also contribute to your overall health. In this chapter, we'll explore three key areas: digestion, sleep, and stress.

Digestion

The importance of gut health for nutrient absorption cannot be overstated. You can eat all the right foods, but if your digestive system isn't functioning optimally, you won't be able to extract and utilize the nutrients effectively.

Here are my 8 strategies you can use to improve gut health:

1) Use unprocessed salt to aid in digestion

I used to avoid salt because I wanted to keep my face from having water retention and look puffy. After discovering that salt was essential for gastric acid, I reincorporated it and it didn't make my face puffy at all.

Salt is a crucial component of gastric acid, which is essential for breaking down food and killing harmful bacteria. Opt for **unprocessed salt** like Celtic sea salt, which contains trace minerals that can support overall health.

2) Allow time between meals for the migrating motor complex (MMC)

The MMC is a pattern of electromechanical activity in your digestive system that occurs between meals. It helps clear out any undigested food particles and bacteria from your stomach and small intestine. To support this process, try to leave at least 3-4 hours between meals without snacking.

If I wake up at 10 a.m. or later in the morning, I have to eat breakfast (because missing breakfast is bad for weight gain and for the body - it creates oxidative stress and our modern environment is already very stressful), so I'll be less hungry than usual for lunch. It would also be disruptive for my digestive system and the MMC. So please, get your digestive system some rest and leave at least 3 hours between meals.

3) Eat foods you enjoy to stimulate digestive juices

Try to remember which foods you liked the most when you were a kid. At that time, there was no food influence and you could exactly know which food you loved. I heard from my parents I loved stealing and eating blue cheese as a baby (I'm French yes) so I believe my instinct don't lie.

When you eat foods you genuinely enjoy, your body anticipates the meal and starts producing digestive juices even before you take your first bite. This can enhance your digestion and nutrient absorption. That's why cooking a good meal at home feels so good.

3) Incorporate collagen/gelatin/glycine-rich foods

These nutrients are not just for glass skin, strong nails, indestructible joints, and gorgeous hair. They are also essential for gut health and can really help to repair the intestinal lining.

Try making delicious stews with oxtail or lamb neck in a slow cooker or an Instant Pot. You can throw in some potatoes with it, carrots, garlic, onions, and ginger, and your entire meal will be ready. I'll share with you my favorite recipes at the end of the book.

These cuts of meat are rich in collagen and gelatin. Lamb's neck is quite cheap even if it is lamb (**the best meat type to gain weight**). Ask your butcher about those cuts. Alternatively, you can supplement with grass-fed collagen powder. I aim for 10-20g of grass-fed collagen powder on days when I don't consume collagen-rich foods.

4) Limit processed food and eating out

Processed foods often contain additives and preservatives that disrupt your gut microbiome. Restaurants may use ingredients that don't agree with your digestive system like seed oils. Learn to cook! It's a valuable life skill that gives you control over what goes into your meals. And you will save some money.

I'm not saying you have to be drastic and ban eating out. If friends ask you to eat with them, don't refuse. The social aspect is very important for digestion! What I'm saying is that if you often resort to ready-made meals out of laziness, it's no coincidence that you don't put on weight, given the lack of nutrition in many ready-made meals.

5) Support digestion

If you have trouble digesting your food, consider supplementing with Betaine HCl or/and drinking a glass of pineapple juice before meals. Pineapple contains bromelain, an enzyme that aids in protein digestion.

When I say 1 glass, it is important. You don't want to drink a lot during a meal as this will dilute your stomach acid and it will be less powerful during digestion. Drink water/juice/milk outside meals when you feel the need. Don't force yourself and listen to your body. Everyone is different. Personally, **I love drinking raw goat's milk between meals with a little strawberry syrup**. It tastes amazing, it is full of good calcium, and excellent for weight gain.

6) Address constipation

I had chronic constipation all my life and I didn't even know. Many people are deficient in magnesium, which can lead to constipation. Try supplementing with magnesium glycinate. This form of magnesium is well-absorbed and can improve bowel movements.

Personally, this was a game-changer for me. I went from having 1 bowel movement a day (sometimes skipping days) to 2-3 bowel movements daily (without diarrhea). Paradoxically, this is when I started to see my weight increase. The more quality bowel movements you have, the better, as it means less stagnant food in your digestive tract, leading to fewer endotoxins. **With fewer bad bacterias in your intestines, you have more power to digest food and absorb nutrients.**

Another trick to address chronic constipation is to drink hot water/infusion between meals. For example, ginger infusion is amazing for this as ginger also improves bowel movements by itself. If you have a thermos, you can pour the ginger infusion inside and drink a bit of it during the day. It's no coincidence that many people in Asia have a little hot liquid with their meals. You can also do it with your meal if you don't drink a lot (see above advice).

7) Try the Ray Peat carrot salad

This simple salad can help lower endotoxins in your gut. It's especially beneficial for women's hormones, but it's also good for men as it can reduce the conversion of testosterone to estrogen. Aim to eat one carrot daily, shredded lengthwise to preserve the good fibers. Serve with coconut oil or extra virgin olive oil, white vinegar or apple cider vinegar, and a pinch of salt. If you can, make sure to eat that at least 45 minutes before your meal cause it can lower the absorption of your food.

By implementing these strategies, you can significantly improve your digestive health, setting a solid foundation for your weight gain journey.

Sleep

Quality sleep is crucial for hormone balance and overall health. It's during sleep that your body repairs tissues, synthesizes proteins, and releases growth hormones - all essential processes for healthy weight gain.

Here are my 4 strategies you can use to optimize your sleep:

1) Try to fall asleep before midnight

The hours of sleep before midnight are more restorative. Try to get to bed early enough to catch these valuable sleep hours. I know it's hard but it's worth it.

Also try to go to bed and wake up at the same time every day, even on weekends. This helps regulate your body's internal clock.

2) Sync with natural light cycles

If possible, try to watch the sunset and sunrise - even if there are some clouds. It's not a problem if you can't see the sun directly. Just try to get this natural light. If you really can't be outside during sunset/sunrise, opening the window and watching the light can also be helpful.

Sunrise light triggers the suprachiasmatic nucleus via blue light, activating the HPA axis and cortisol production, crucial for adrenal health and circadian rhythm regulation (which governs your sleep-wake cycle.)

Sunset light signals the body to prepare for rest by reducing cortisol and stimulating melatonin production, which is vital for sleep. This warm light enhances circadian rhythm alignment, promoting hormonal balance and relaxation. Sunset viewing also activates the parasympathetic nervous system, fostering calmness and healing, essential for a smooth transition into a restful sleep.

Post sunset, you need to wear blue light glasses to not disrupt the pineal melatonin production. Use a warm lighting bulb in the evening and enable the night shift on your smartphone and on your screens. You'll find a link to warm bulbs and glasses on the resources page.

3) Create a pre-sleep routine

Try to disconnect from work completely before sleeping. A good way to wind down is to read a **fiction book** or watch a relaxing movie (with night shift enabled on your screen and wearing your blue light-blocking glasses).

Progressive muscle relaxation can be also very effective. You'll find a follow-along video about this technique on the resource page.

Limit caffeine and alcohol: Both can disrupt sleep quality. Try to avoid caffeine after 2 pm and limit alcohol consumption, especially close to bedtime. On the other hand, taking a magnesium supplement or having a **chamomile infusion** before sleeping can be very helpful to fall asleep quickly.

4) Optimize your sleep environment:

Ensure your bedroom is dark, quiet, and cool. Consider using blackout curtains and keeping the temperature around 65°F (18°C) for optimal sleep.

By prioritizing sleep, you're giving your body the best chance to repair, grow, and utilize the nutrients you're consuming for healthy weight gain.

Stress

Chronic stress can significantly impact your ability to gain weight. It affects nutrient absorption, disrupts sleep, and can even increase calorie burning.

Here are 6 techniques to reduce stress and improve your body's response to weight gain efforts:

1) Exercise regularly / play an instrument

Physical activity is a great stress reliever. It doesn't have to be intense. If you're playing an instrument, make sure to keep this hobby because it's a very powerful activity to mitigate stress.

2) Practice breathing

Deep, diaphragmatic breathing can activate your body's relaxation response. Try the 4—5-7 technique for beginners: inhale for 4 counts, hold for 5, and exhale for 7. There's an app called State that's amazing for that.

3) Limit screen time

Constant connectivity can be a source of stress. Especially watching the dreamy fake life of complete strangers on Instagram or TikTok. Set boundaries around your use of phones and computers, especially before bedtime.

Use apps such as Jomo to limit your screentime:

CHAPTER 3 - BEFORE STARTING YOUR WEIGHT GAIN JOURNEY, FIX...

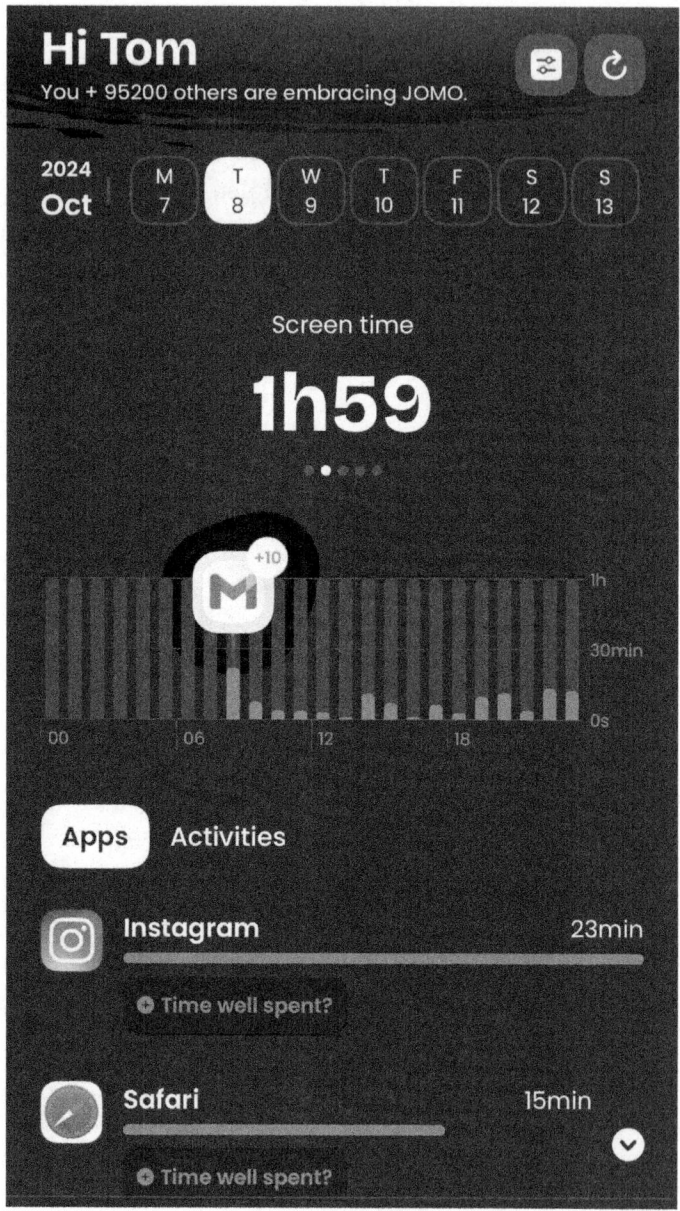

4) Do a quick vagus nerve reset:

The vagus nerve plays a crucial role in your parasympathetic nervous system, which controls your "rest and digest" state.

A simple way to stimulate the vagus nerve is to do the butterfly technique. I like to do it before sleeping and sometimes before lunch or dinner.

Here's how it works: standing, sitting or lying down, look with your eyes to the left without turning your head. Hold this position. You'll see that this will make you yawn after a few tens of seconds. Once you feel this, now look to the left without moving your head and wait for a sign of deep relaxation such as yawning or swallowing. That's it! It's quick but highly effective. You'll find an explanatory video on the resources page.

5) Connect with others

Social support is crucial for managing stress. Make time for friends and family, or consider joining a hobby social group. When I'm in a new city, for example, I like to go skateboarding or go to the street workout park cause you always meet people naturally.

6) Get out in nature

Spending time in green spaces reduces stress levels. Try to incorporate regular walks in parks or other natural settings into your routine. Managing stress is not just about implementing these techniques when you feel overwhelmed. It's about creating a lifestyle that inherently reduces stress.

By addressing digestion, sleep, and stress - you're setting yourself up for success in your weight gain journey. These foundational elements of health will not only support your efforts to gain weight but will also contribute to your overall health. It's not just about gaining weight, but about gaining health and vitality in the process.

In the next chapter, we'll finally dive into the specifics of nutrition for healthy weight gain.

Chapter 4 - 3 Rules to Master for Gaining Weight

Gaining weight isn't just about eating more; it's about eating right. In this chapter, we'll explore three fundamental rules for a successful and sustainable weight gain. These rules will help you not just increase your body mass but do so in a way that promotes overall health.

Rule n*1: Eat More Calories than You Burn

The first and most basic rule of weight gain is to consume more calories than your body burns. This creates a caloric and energy surplus, which your body can use to build new tissue, including muscle and fat. However, it's crucial to approach this mindfully, balancing quantity with quality.

Calculate calorie needs without compromising food quality

To start, you need to understand your baseline caloric needs. This is known as your Total Daily Energy Expenditure (TDEE). You can calculate this using online calculators that take into account your age, gender, height, weight, and activity level. Once you know your TDEE, aim to consume 300-500 calories above this number daily for steady weight gain.

For example, if your TDEE is 2500 calories, you should aim for 2800-3000 calories per day. This moderate surplus is enough to promote weight gain without overwhelming your digestive system or leading to excessive fat gain.

Use the Cronometer app to count your calories. If you see you're gaining weight, continue with the same plan. If you're stagnating or not gaining weight, increase your calories slightly. Counting calories is a pain at first, but do it until you start gaining weight, and you'll get a good idea of how many calories and energy you're getting from the food you eat. The Cronometer app is also great for showing you what vitamins and minerals you've consumed at the end of the day. This can be very useful in uncovering deficiencies.

However, it's crucial to remember that not all calories are created equal. **While you're increasing your caloric intake, focus on whole, nutrient-dense foods** rather than processed, high-calorie options. This approach ensures that you're not just gaining weight, but doing so in a way that supports your health and doesn't destroy your gut.

If you struggle to eat large meals, try eating 4-5 smaller meals throughout the day instead of 3 large ones.

Remember, the goal is to gain weight gradually and healthily. Rapid weight gain is more likely to result in fat accumulation rather than muscle growth.

Rule n*2: Avoid empty and negative calories

While creating a caloric surplus is important, the quality of those calories matters just as much. Focusing on nutrient-dense foods ensures that your body gets the building blocks and the energy it needs for healthy weight gain.

Empty and negative calories come from highly processed foods, and foods with unhealthy fats (PUFA oils are everywhere in industrialized food). They are low in nutrients and full of anti-nutrients. While these foods can help you meet your calorie goals, they don't provide the nutrients your body needs for optimal function and healthy weight gain.

Examples of empty and negative calorie foods include:

- **Processed foods** like chips, noodles and cookies
- **Fast food:** But a homemade burger with grass-fed beef patty can be excellent for weight gain.
- **Vegetables:** Sorry for all vegans out there but if you want

to gain weight, avoid vegies. They can be difficult to digest, especially when you're already trying to increase your calories. They don't provide much energy, so it's not worth it. I still eat vegetables, but more to enhance the taste of my dishes. I use garlic and onions in many of my dishes, but also carrots, tomatoes, and celery in my glycine-rich meat broths. So you can eat vegetables, but keep them at the bare minimum. Fruits, however, are very good for a dessert. We'll talk about this later.

- **Legumes like beans and lentils**: These are full of anti-nutrients that can disrupt mineral absorption, leading to bloating and digestive discomfort. They appear to be high in protein, but this is far less assimilated by the body than protein from dairy or animal products. I chose to focus on this type of protein at the start of my weight gain adventure and my gut paid the consequences...
- **Alcohol:** beer is the worst but occasional wine, tequila, and vodka can be fine if your liver is in good health.
- **Whole grains**: their high fiber content can irritate the digestive system, slowing down digestion and preventing the absorption of necessary calories.
- **Polyunsaturated oils:** such as sunflower, rapeseed, linseed, peanut, walnut, or sesame. They disrupt metabolism, increase inflammation and inhibit the production of hormones needed for weight gain.
- **Nuts**: These include almonds, walnuts, hazelnuts, etc. Their high content of unsaturated polysaccharides can once again disrupt your metabolism by inhibiting thyroid function. They are often difficult to digest, and they contain anti-nutrients that block the absorption of essential minerals such as zinc or magnesium, which are necessary

for muscle growth and regeneration. One exception is Brazil nuts, which are a good source of selenium if soaked the day before in vinegar water to remove anti-nutrients.

While these foods can be enjoyed occasionally for social connections, they shouldn't form the basis of your weight gain diet. Focus on foods that are not only calorie-dense but also rich in nutrients. Your body will have the resources it needs to build muscle, support bone health, maintain a strong immune system, and keep all bodily functions running smoothly. The next chapter will show you what these foods are in each category: carbs, proteins, fats, dairy products, vegetables, fruits, etc.

Rule n*3: Consistency is Key

The third rule for successful weight gain is consistency. **Weight gain, like any body composition change, takes time.** It's not something that happens overnight or even over a few weeks. **It requires patience, persistence, and consistency in your eating habits.**

The hardest part is staying consistent. And you'll see that if you deviate for a few days, you'll lose a little weight straight away thanks to your fast metabolism…

A friend of mine was naturally skinny but managed to put on 20kg in just a few years! One day we traveled to Mexico and he fell ill with dengue fever for ten days, during which time he was unable to eat every meal. He immediately lost 15kg. Thanks to muscle memory and a good diet, he was able to regain the lost kilos and muscles within a few months.

This illustrates well the importance of being consistent when you are able to, because a small deviation of a few days can change everything. The situation in the story is extreme, I admit, but you get the idea.

But don't worry, over time, consistent eating becomes a habit, making it easier to maintain your weight gain diet long-term.

Chapter 5 - Best Foods to Gain Weight

As we saw, not all foods are created equal. Some food categories are particularly effective for weight gain, providing not just calories but also essential nutrients. In this chapter, we'll explore the best food categories for weight gain and highlight specific foods within each category that can help you reach your goals.

Proteins

Protein is essential for building muscle mass and supporting overall health. When it comes to weight gain, the source and quality of protein matter significantly.

Animal proteins are more easily digested and absorbed than plant proteins

Animal proteins are considered complete proteins, containing all essential amino acids in the right proportions. They're also more bioavailable, meaning your body can utilize them more efficiently. This makes animal proteins superior for weight gain compared to plant proteins.

Fattier protein sources are more effective for weight gain. When aiming to gain weight, fattier cuts of meat can be particularly beneficial as they provide both protein and additional calories from fat. Some excellent options include:

- **TOP - Lamb**: Shoulder and neck cuts. Lamb can be expensive but lamb neck is actually cheap and full of glycine and collagen.
- **Very good - Beef**: Oxtail, ground beef, osso buco, entrecote, chuck square cut. Overall better than chicken because it is more nutrient-dense.
- **Very good - Fish:** Sardines (big fish like salmon are often contaminated with heavy metals)
- **Good - Pork**: Belly, shoulder
- **Good - Duck and chicken:** Roasted chicken or duck with skin. Duck is superior to chicken but it is less common. If one day you're in a Vietnamese restaurant, ask for a Duck Phở soup it's amazing.

These fattier cuts not only provide more calories but also tend to be more flavorful, which can help stimulate appetite. In today's society, we eat a lot of lean proteins such as low fat ground beef or chicken breast. But it's also important to eat gelatinous meat (oxtail, lamb neck...) rich in **glycine** and other amino acids, as our grandparents did. This will ensure a balanced supply of amino acids and avoid the harmful effects of excess cysteine and tryptophan found in lean meat.

Hierarchy of protein sources from most to least calorie-dense:

1. **Fatty cuts of red meat (lamb, beef)**
2. **Whole eggs (pasture-raised eggs only)**
3. **Full-fat dairy (raw milk, cheese)**
4. **Fatty fish (sardines, mackerel)**
5. **Poultry with skin**
6. **Pork**

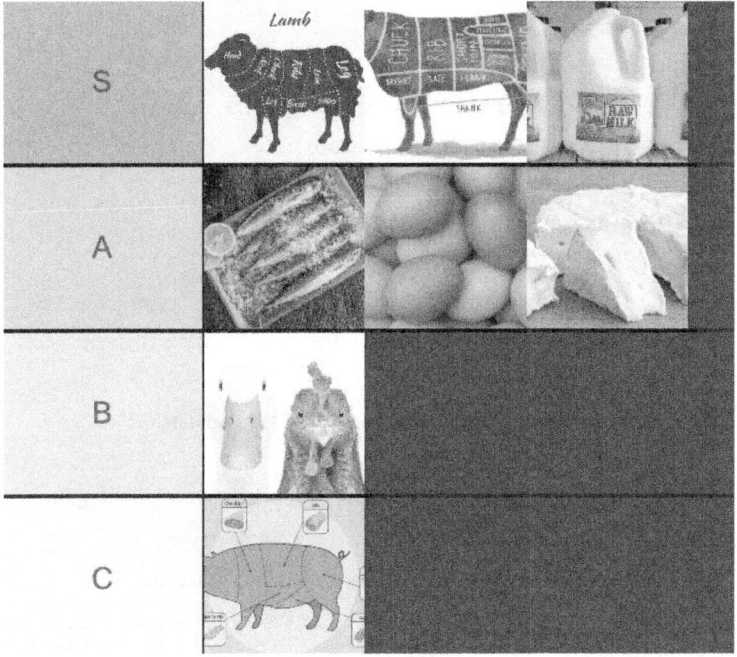

Remember, while this hierarchy is based on calorie density, it's important to include a variety of protein sources in your diet to ensure you're getting a wide range of nutrients.

Dairy

Dairy products can be excellent for weight gain, providing a mix of protein, fats, and carbohydrates along with important micronutrients like calcium and vitamin D.

Raw dairy products, which haven't undergone pasteurization, offer several benefits:

1. Contains natural enzymes that aid digestion
2. May be better tolerated by some people who have difficulty with pasteurized dairy
3. Retain more of their natural nutrients

However, it's important to source raw dairy from reputable, clean sources to minimize the risk of foodborne illness.

Here's the hierarchy of the best dairy products:

- **TOP - Raw milk**: Contains enzymes that aid digestion and is often better tolerated than pasteurized milk
- **TOP - Raw A2 milk**: May be easier to digest for some people
- **TOP - Raw Goat milk**: Even easier to digest than cow's milk
- **TOP - Raw Camel milk**: Rich in nutrients and potentially beneficial for those with dairy sensitivities

- **Very good - Cheese**: Especially aged cheeses (Emmental-Brie-Roquefort-Tomme-Beaufort-Comté-Parmegiano). For a snack, a nice piece of cheese with some raw honey is amazing.
- **Very good - Raw cream**

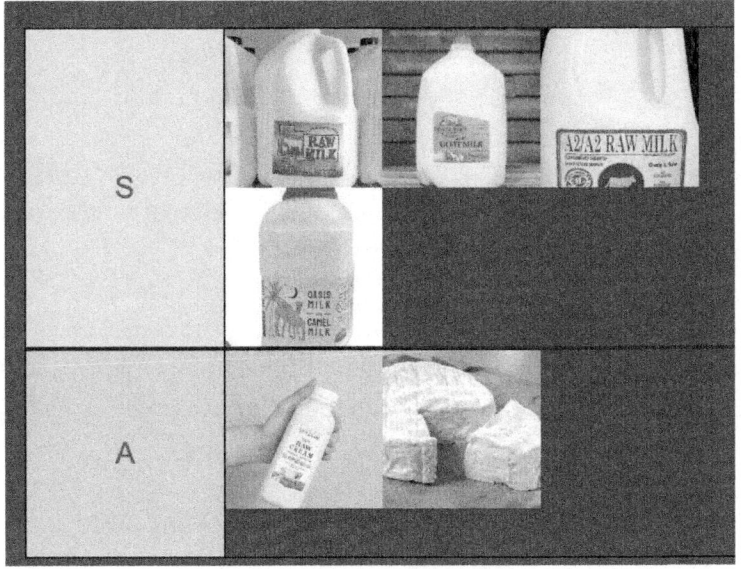

Here are some ways to include dairy in your weight-gain diet:

- Drink milk between meals. Did you know that milk is even more hydrating than water?
- Add cheese to your meals for extra calories and flavor. Grated Parmigiano, pecorino, or even compté is amazing over pasta and stews.

- Incorporate cream into your cooking (e.g., in sauces or soups)

Remember, if you're lactose intolerant, you might still be able to tolerate certain dairy products like hard cheeses or goat milk.

Fats

Fats are crucial for weight gain due to their high caloric density. One gram of fat provides 9 calories, compared to 4 calories per gram for both protein and carbohydrates.

Including healthy fats in your diet is one of the easiest ways to increase your calorie intake without having to eat large volumes of food. This is particularly beneficial for those with smaller appetites.

Fats can come from two main sources in your diet:

1. Fats naturally present in protein sources: Such as the marbling in a steak or the fat in whole milk
2. Pure fat sources: Such as olive oil, butter, ghee, or lard

Both can be beneficial for weight gain, but pure fat sources allow you to easily add extra calories to your meals.

Animal fats are more similar in structure to human body fat, making them easier for our bodies to utilize. **Hierarchy of**

excellent sources of animal fats:

1. **Butter (preferably from grass-fed cows)**
2. **Coconut oil**
3. **Ghee**
4. **Beef tallow**
5. **Extra virgin olive oil (needs to come from a good source)**
6. **Lard**
7. **Duck fat**

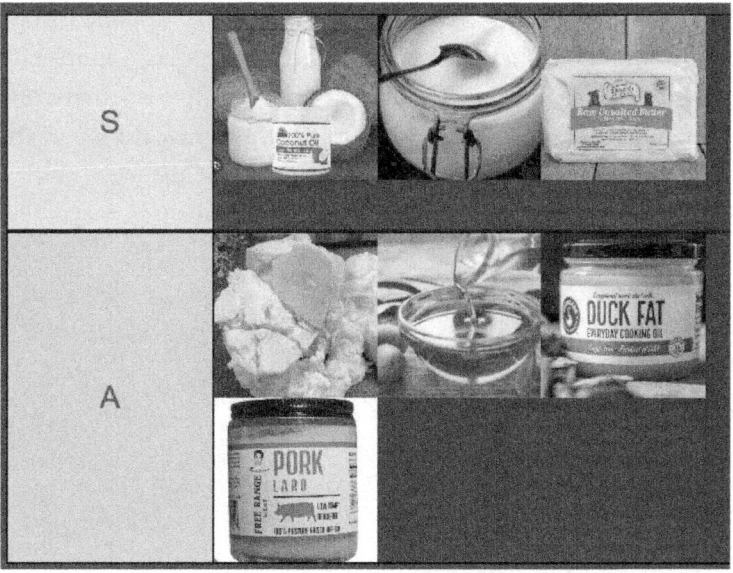

If you're not used to fat, go slowly. Don't put too much at first. For a starter, a bit of butter on top of warm rice tastes really good. Also, if you're eating lamb, no need to add fat as it is already very fatty.

Carbohydrates

Carbohydrates are your body's primary energy source and play a crucial role in weight gain by providing calories and stimulating insulin secretion, which helps with nutrient absorption and storage.

Carbohydrates are quickly converted to glucose in your body, providing readily available energy. They also stimulate insulin secretion, which helps shuttle nutrients (including amino acids from protein) into your cells, supporting muscle growth and weight gain. For this reason, **take 1-2 tbp of raw honey at the end of each meal**. This small habit is a very small effort, yet, it will be very effective for your weight gain journey.

Hierarchy of carb sources:

1. **Raw honey**
2. **Dried fruits (dates, figs, raisins)**
3. **Fruits**
4. **White rice**
5. **Potatoes (white, sweet)**
6. **Ancient grains (sorghum, amaranth, millet)**

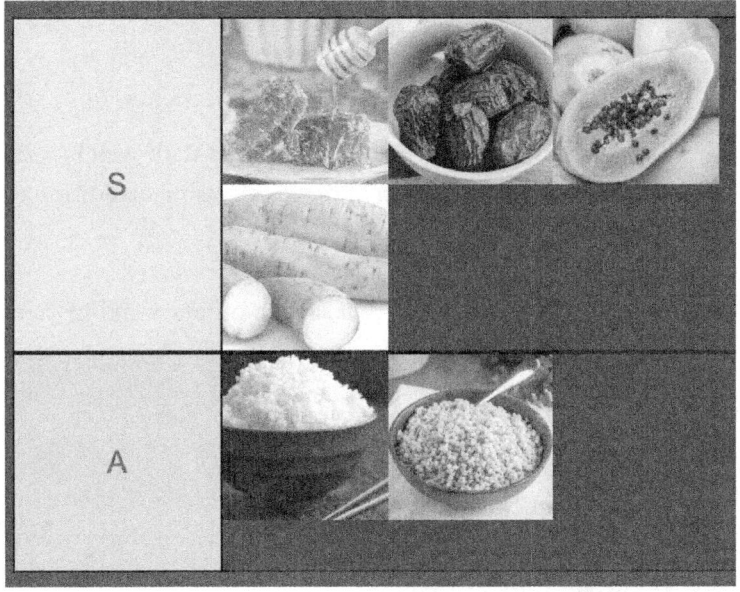

Importance of raw honey as a superior carb source:

Raw honey deserves special mention as a superior carbohydrate source for weight gain. It's not only calorie-dense but also rich in enzymes, antioxidants, and other beneficial compounds. Raw honey can aid digestion, support immune function, and provide quick energy. Don't forget your tbsp of raw honey at the end of each meal!

Vegetables

While vegetables are not typically associated with weight gain due to their low-calorie density, they can be a nice addition to your meals.

Some vegetables are easier to digest than others, making them better choices when you're trying to gain weight. Easy-to-digest vegetables include:

1. **Cooked carrots**
2. **Cooked zucchini**
3. **Cooked sweet potatoes**
4. **Cooked pumpkin**
5. **Cooked celery**

Onions, ginger, and garlic are also very good for the stomach but not in excess for garlic.

Impact of cooking on nutrient content

Overcooking often has negative effects on nutrient content:
 - Heat destroy some vitamins, particularly water-soluble vitamins like vitamin C and some B vitamins
 - Some cooking methods can add nutrients, like calcium when bones are cooked in a stew

Try not to cook your food in non-stick stoves or pans. They're very bad for your health once they've been damaged. This can overload your toxin elimination system and slow down your digestion.

Glass is the healthiest material. So **try Vision frying pans and saucepans**. A link will be on the resources page. I also use Instant Pot a lot for meat broths and stews with lamb neck and oxtail.

Micronutrients and vitamins

While macronutrients (proteins, fats, and carbohydrates) provide the bulk of your calories, micronutrients (vitamins and minerals) are crucial for overall health and optimal functioning of your body.

Micronutrients play various roles in the body that support healthy weight gain:

- **B vitamins** are crucial for energy metabolism
- **Vitamin D and calcium** support bone health as you gain weight
- **Iron** is essential for oxygen transport, supporting increased muscle mass
- **Zinc** plays a role in protein synthesis and wound healing
- **Magnesium** is involved in muscle and nerve function

Here are some of the best food sources for important micronutrients:

1. **Vitamin A:** Liver, heart (I try to consume them weekly because it's literally a multivitamin - lamb liver is tastier than beef liver)
2. **B vitamins:** Meat, eggs, dairy
3. **Vitamin C:** Citrus fruits, bell peppers
4. **Vitamin D:** Sardines, egg yolks, mushrooms (and sunlight

exposure)
5. **Vitamin E:** Eggs, mango, red bell pepper, liver
6. **Vitamin K:** Cheese, and Japanese natto if you can handle it
7. **Calcium:** Dairy products, sardines, leafy greens
8. **Iron:** Red meat, organ meats
9. **Zinc:** Oysters, beef
10. **Magnesium**: Milk, orange juice, chocolate

Now you know the best foods for healthy weight gain. It may sound complicated, but in the next chapter, I'm going to give you some meal ideas using these foods, so you can use them every day to start gaining weight.

By focusing on nutrient-dense whole foods, you can ensure you're getting a wide range of micronutrients to support your weight gain goals. Remember to include a variety of foods in your diet to ensure you're getting a wide range of nutrients. Let's check the best weight gain recipes now!

Chapter 6 - Weight Gain Meal Plan for 1 Week

This meal plan is designed to provide a substantial calorie surplus while focusing on nutrient-dense, whole foods. You'll notice a variety of protein sources, plenty of healthy fats, and a good balance of carbohydrates. I've also included my favorite snacks and desserts to help increase overall calorie intake.

Remember, this is just an example and may need to be adjusted based on the meat cuts you can find, your digestion, and most importantly, if you see that you're gaining weight too fast/too slow. The portion sizes provided are estimates and can be scaled up or down depending on your specific calorie requirements.

Use this plan to inspire your meal planning. As you become more comfortable with the principles of healthy weight gain, you'll be able to create your own varied and enjoyable meal plans that support your goals.

Monday

- **Breakfast**: 2 bananas cooked in coconut oil with cinnamon

powder + 3 pasture-raised eggs
- **Lunch**: Spaghetti alla bolognese (5.3 oz spaghetti + 6.3 oz ground beef in 5.3 oz tomato sauce + parmigiano/pecorino cheese). 1 apple as dessert
- **Snack**: 3 or more Medjool dates with cheese (3.5 oz) and honey (2 tbsp)
- **Dinner**: Lamb neck stew (8.8 oz lamb) with potatoes (8.8 oz). Coconut ice cream (3.5 oz) as dessert

Tuesday

- **Breakfast**: 1.8 oz of raw goat's cheese with 2 eggs and 3.5 oz of blueberries
- **Lunch**: Rice (4.2 oz dry weight) cooked in lamb meat broth with roasted chicken (7 oz). 1 orange as dessert
- **Snack**: Ray Peat carrot salad (1 large carrot, 5.3 oz)
- **Dinner**: Lamb leftovers with broth and semolina (3 oz). Add honey (2 tbsp) and dry raisins for some Moroccan vibes. 1 pear as dessert

Wednesday

- **Breakfast**: Raisins (3.5 oz), 3 pasture-raised eggs, and 2 tbsp honey
- **Lunch**: Oxtail (8.8 oz) with celery (3.5 oz) and potatoes (8.8 oz). 1 apple as dessert
- **Snack**: Greek yogurt (7 oz) with raspberries (3.5 oz) and 2 tbsp honey
- **Dinner**: Osso buco (8.8 oz) with rice (4.2 oz dry weight) cooked in meat broth. Homemade coconut ice cream (3.5 oz) as dessert

Thursday

- **Breakfast**: 3 pasture-raised eggs with roasted chicken leftovers
- **Lunch**: Spaghetti (5.3 oz) with mussels (7 oz). Dried fruits as dessert
- **Snack**: Papaya cream (I'll show you the recipe later in the book)
- **Dinner**: Bone broth rice (4.2 oz dry weight) with sardines (5.3 oz). 1 fresh fruit as dessert

Friday

- **Breakfast**: 2 bananas cooked in coconut oil (0.5 oz) with cinnamon powder + 3 pasture-raised eggs
- **Lunch**: Lamb or veal liver (7 oz) with onions (3.5 oz) and 2 tbsp honey + potatoes (8.8 oz). 1 fresh fruit as dessert
- **Snack**: Ray Peat carrot salad (1 carrot)
- **Dinner**: Bone broth rice (4.2 oz dry weight) with ground beef (6.3 oz) and caramelized onions. 1 apple as dessert

Saturday

- **Breakfast**: 1.8 oz of raw goat's cheese with 2 eggs and 3.5 oz of blueberries
- **Lunch**: Chuck square cut beef (8.8 oz) with meat broth rice (4.2 oz dry weight). 1 orange as dessert
- **Snack**: 3 or more Medjool dates with cheese (3.5 oz) and 2 tbsp honey
- **Dinner**: Potatoes (8.8 oz) cooked in oven + cheese on top with a beef patty (6.3 oz). Cooked applesauce (7 oz) with

cinnamon as dessert

Sunday

- **Breakfast**: Papaya cream
- **Lunch**: Lamb shoulder (8.8 oz) with sweet potatoes (8.8 oz). Greek yogurt (7 oz) with honey (2 tbsp) as dessert
- **Snack**: Milkshake (1 egg + 3.2 oz raw milk + 1.9 oz raw cream + 2 tbsp honey)
- **Dinner**: Osso buco (8.8 oz) with rice (4.2 oz dry weight) cooked in meat broth. Homemade coconut ice cream (3.5 oz) and 1 pear as dessert

The recipes for specific dishes like the papaya cream, milkshake, and Ray Peat carrot salad will be detailed in Chapter 10.

This meal plan is literally your roadmap to successful weight gain. Trust the process. It provides a solid foundation for your weight gain journey, but it's also important to be aware of potential pitfalls along the way. Even with the best intentions, many people make common mistakes that can hinder their progress. In the next chapter, we'll explore these frequent missteps and how you can avoid them.

Chapter 7 - Common mistakes

At the start of your weight gain journey, it's easy to fall into certain traps that can hinder your progress. In this chapter, we'll explore some of the most common mistakes people make when trying to gain weight, and how to avoid them.

Eating too much protein and not enough carbs/fats

One of the most frequent mistakes in weight gain diets is overemphasizing protein while neglecting carbohydrates and fats. While protein is crucial for muscle building, it's not the most efficient nutrient for weight gain.

Protein has a high thermic effect, meaning your body burns more calories digesting it compared to carbs or fats. Additionally, excess protein that isn't used for muscle building or other bodily functions is not easily stored and can be converted to glucose through a process called gluconeogenesis.

To avoid this mistake:

1. Aim for a balanced macronutrient ratio. A good starting point is 30% protein, 40% carbohydrates, and 30% fats.
2. Include a source of carbohydrates and healthy fats with each meal. 1 tbsp of extra virgin olive oil on each meal is a good place to start. Butter on rice is amazing too.
3. Don't shy away from fattier cuts of meat like lamb neck or full-fat dairy products like raw goat milk.

Remember, your body needs energy to build muscle and gain weight. **Carbohydrates and fats provide this energy more efficiently than protein**.

Avoiding breakfast

Skipping breakfast is a common habit, especially for those who aren't naturally big eaters. However, this can be a significant obstacle to weight gain.

Breakfast kick-starts your metabolism and sets the tone for your eating habits throughout the day. When you skip breakfast, you miss out on a key opportunity to add calories to your daily intake.

To make the most of breakfast:

1. Prepare calorie-dense, easy-to-eat breakfast options. Think eggs, milk, fruits, or even ice cream.
2. If you're not hungry in the morning, start with something small and gradually increase portion sizes.

3. Make breakfast a non-negotiable part of your routine, even if it means waking up a bit earlier.

Consuming too many indigestible foods

In an attempt to eat "clean" or increase fiber intake, many people overloads with foods that are difficult to digest. These often include raw vegetables, whole grains, and legumes. **Consuming them frequently can lead to digestive discomfort and make it harder to meet your calorie goals**.

They're low in calories and high in fiber, which can make you feel full without contributing significantly to your calorie intake. Plus, as we saw a lot of those contain anti-nutrients.

Don't eliminate them, but don't let them dominate your plate.

Ignoring gut health

Your digestive system plays a crucial role in your ability to gain weight. If your gut isn't healthy, you won't be able to properly absorb the nutrients from the food you're eating, no matter how much you consume.

Listen to your stomach, and remember that the quality of your stools indicates good intestinal health. If you go to the toilet more than 2 times and your poo is neither too hard nor too soft, and you don't need to work hard to get it out, then this is a very good indication of excellent intestinal health.

If not, try to improve your intestinal health with the 10 advice I gave you in Chapter 3:

1. Incorporate collagen/gelatin/glycine-rich foods (e.g., oxtail, lamb neck) Consider supplementing with grass-fed collagen powder if you can't get those cuts,
2. Allow 3-4 hours between meals for the migrating motor complex (MMC),
3. Support digestion with Betaine HCl or pineapple juice during meals,
4. Don't drink too much during meals to avoid diluting stomach acid,
5. Address constipation with magnesium glycinate supplements,
6. Use unprocessed salt (like Celtic sea salt) to aid digestion,
7. Try the Ray Peat carrot salad to lower endotoxins,
8. Eat foods you enjoy to stimulate digestive juices,
9. Drink hot water/ginger infusion between meals,
10. Limit processed food and eating out.

Lack of patience

Weight gain, especially muscle gain, is a slow process. Many people become discouraged when they don't see immediate results and give up too soon. Remember, healthy and sustainable weight gain typically occurs at a rate of 0.5-1 pound (0.2-0.4 kg) per week.

Setting goals in mind is a good thing, but don't give up hope if you see that you're not reaching them quickly. It's a marathon, not a sprint. You need to be consistent over several weeks, months, and years, and avoid missing the mark several days in a row, and then you'll see results.

And don't forget to track your progress! This will motivate you. You can take photos of your body and put them in a special album, but also log your weight in a notebook with the date or use an app like MY Weight.

Avoiding these common mistakes can significantly improve your weight gain journey.

By being mindful of these potential pitfalls, you can create a more effective and sustainable approach to weight gain. In the next chapter, we'll explore the best supplements to support weight gain and your overall health. They're not magic pills for weight gain, but some have helped me enormously and I still use them today.

Chapter 8 - Best Supplements to Support Weight Gain

Certain supplements can enhance nutrient absorption and support gut health. They will improve your digestion and the absorbency of your meals. Many naturally skinny people have problems in this area.

Below are the supplements that have helped me the most, starting with the most useful. Perhaps you'll find supplements that align with the problems you're having.

On the resources page, you'll find the best sources of all these supplements, because not all are created equal, and their quality is extremely important if you don't want to throw money away.

Magnesium Glycinate: Supporting digestive health and bowel movements

Magnesium is an essential mineral involved in over 300 enzymatic reactions in the body. Magnesium glycinate is a highly bioavailable form that's gentle on the stomach.

Benefits:

- Supports healthy digestion and regular bowel movements

- Aids in protein synthesis and energy production
- Promotes relaxation and better sleep quality
- May help reduce muscle cramps and tension

Dosage: 200-400mg daily, preferably in the evening. Start with a lower dose and increase gradually to avoid loose stools.

I used to be constipated but magnesium glycinate has solved this problem and since the days I started taking it, I have 2 to 4 bowel movements a day.

Suffering from acne all over my body, in just a few days my acne gradually disappeared. All that food that used to stagnate in my stomach and had to be detoxified somehow was detoxified via my skin, the last emunctory in the detoxification system. That's why it's important to have several bowel movements a day, especially when building mass, but also to sweat!

Beef/Goat Colostrum: Gut health and immune support

CHAPTER 8 - BEST SUPPLEMENTS TO SUPPORT WEIGHT GAIN

Colostrum is the first milk produced by mammals after giving birth. It's rich in antibodies, growth factors, and nutrients that support immune function and gut health.

Benefits:

- Supports gut lining repair and integrity
- Boosts immune function
- Contains growth factors like IGF-1, which support muscle growth
- Rich in proteins, vitamins, and minerals

Dosage: 1-3 grams daily on an empty stomach. Start with a lower dose to assess tolerance. Take it when you wake up on an empty stomach.

I feel that colostrum also stimulates a bit of bowel movements but not as much as magnesium. Colostrum is excellent for immunity because it contains lactoferrin (which shapes babies' immunity when they don't have any at the start). You'll get much less sick with this supplement, really!

I've also noticed that it makes my body **slightly more robust and masculine** (thanks to the slight IGF-1 in the colostrum, I presume). In women too, I've heard that their curves appear more feminine when they take colostrum. Last but not least, it's excellent for acne, particularly persistent back acne, as it repairs not only the skin but also the mucous membranes (including the intestinal lining).

Grass-fed collagen: Repairing gut lining

CHAPTER 8 - BEST SUPPLEMENTS TO SUPPORT WEIGHT GAIN

Collagen plays a crucial role in gut health. Grass-fed collagen is the best type of collagen.

Benefits:

- Supports gut lining repair and integrity
- May improve skin elasticity and hydration
- Supports joint health and can reduce joint pain
- Can enhance muscle mass when combined with resistance training

Dosage: Aim for 10-20 grams daily if you don't consume

gelatin-rich meat cuts regularly.

At first, I took collagen to preserve my joints when I began to go to the gym. But later, I discovered that it was **extremely important for rebuilding the intestinal lining**. The quality of hair, skin, and nails also improves with collagen consumption.

I mix it most often in Greek yogurt or my ginger or chamomile infusion. Today, I try to eat cuts of meat that contain a lot of collagen (oxtail, lamb's neck…) almost every day. On days when that's not the case, or when I'm out of town, I take 10-20g of collagen a day.

Dandelion tincture: Supporting liver function

CHAPTER 8 - BEST SUPPLEMENTS TO SUPPORT WEIGHT GAIN

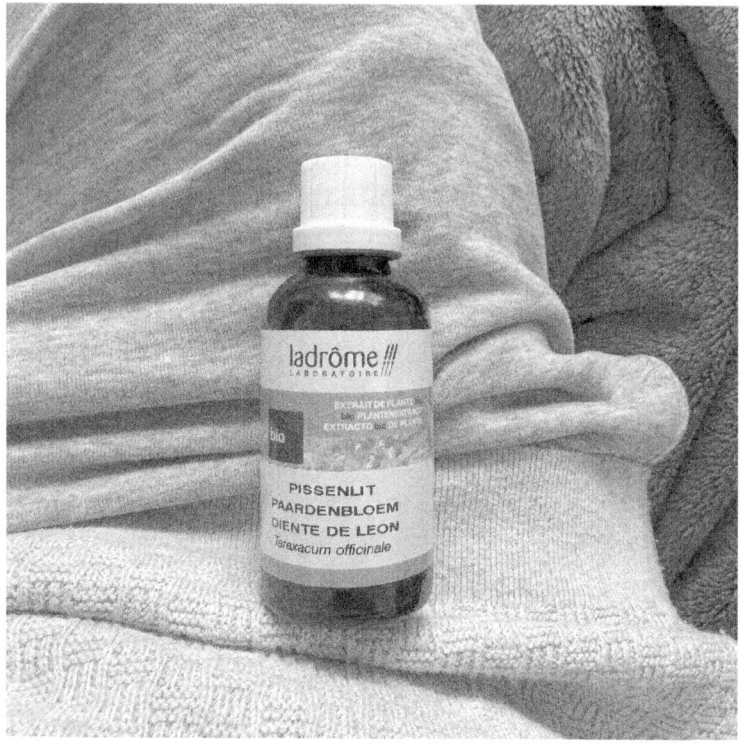

Dandelion has been used for centuries in traditional medicine to support liver health and detoxification. A tincture is a concentrated liquid extract that's easy to use.

Benefits:

- Supports liver detoxification processes
- May improve skin health by supporting the body's natural detox pathways
- Can stimulate bile production, aiding in fat digestion
- Has diuretic properties, supporting kidney function

Dosage: Follow the instructions on the product label. Take it just before sleeping.

A healthy liver will enhance your ability to absorb what you eat and detoxify your body, which is already overloaded with toxins due to the environment we live in today. The fewer toxins you have, the easier it will be to gain weight, as your body will be able to focus on your goal.

Betaine HCL: Improving digestion

Betaine Hydrochloride (HCL) supplements can be beneficial for those with low stomach acid, a condition that can impair protein digestion and nutrient absorption.

Benefits:

- Increases stomach acid production, aiding protein digestion
- Improve absorption of vitamins and minerals, especially B12, iron, and calcium
- Can help reduce symptoms of indigestion, bloating, and fullness

Dosage: Start with one capsule (usually 350-750mg) with protein-rich meals. Gradually increase the dose until you feel a warm sensation in your stomach, then reduce it by one capsule. This is not a medical advice.

Betaine can be very useful for kick-starting weight gain and boosting digestion. It will get your body used to the larger quantities you need to digest.

Royal Jelly: Enhancing nutrient absorption and overall vitality

Royal jelly is a nutrient-rich substance produced by worker

bees for the queen bee. It's packed with proteins, vitamins, minerals, and unique compounds that can boost overall health and nutrient absorption.

Benefits:

- Enhances protein absorption, crucial for muscle growth
- Rich in B-complex vitamins, supporting energy metabolism
- Contains unique fatty acids that may improve skin health and wound healing
- May boost immune function and reduce inflammation

Dosage: 1g so 0,2 teaspoons. This is really important because too much can be fatal. People like to take it on an empty stomach in the morning but I like to take it with lunch to enhance protein absorption.

Coconut water (if you live in the tropics): Natural electrolytes and micronutrients

While not a supplement in the traditional sense, coconut water is a natural source of electrolytes and micronutrients that can support hydration and overall health.

If you live in tropical areas like Mexico or Hawaï, you know that you can find fresh coconuts on every corner of the street. If it's your case, don't neglect coconut water, it's a treat!

Benefits:

- Rich in potassium, magnesium, and sodium
- Natural source of B-vitamins
- Can support hydration, especially post-workout
- May help balance electrolytes

Fenugreek: Benefits for women

Fenugreek has a long history of use in Africa and the Middle East. It's known for its potential to increase weight in women when they reach marriageable age.

Benefits:

- Stimulate appetite
- Increase breast size due to its phytoestrogen content
- Help balance blood sugar levels

Dosage: Typically 500-1000mg of fenugreek seed powder daily. Always consult with a healthcare provider before use, especially if pregnant or breastfeeding.

Note: Fenugreek is generally not recommended for men due to its potential estrogenic effects, which could interfere with testosterone levels.

While these supplements can be beneficial, they should complement, not replace, a nutritious whole-food diet. Start with lower doses and gradually increase to assess tolerance and effectiveness.

Chapter 9 - Sport and Activity to Gain Weight

Incorporating the right type and amount of physical activity is crucial. The goal is to stimulate muscle growth and overall strength without burning excessive calories or creating too much metabolic stress.

This chapter will guide you through effective workout strategies for both women and men, as well as provide tips on post-workout nutrition to support your weight gain goals.

For Men: Gym or Calisthenics

For men, focusing on compound exercises either in the gym or through calisthenics can be highly effective for gaining weight and building muscle mass.

When working out in the gym, focus on compound exercises that engage multiple muscle groups simultaneously. This approach stimulates more muscle fibers and promotes overall growth. Here are some excellent exercises:

- **Squats**
- **Deadlifts (have a very good form)**
- **Bench press**
- **Overhead press**
- **Rows**
- **Pull-ups or lat pulldowns**

I started going to the gym with friends but now I prefer to do some calisthenics because I enjoy it better. You can do it shirtless with sun exposure and in my case, in front of the Mediterranean sea!

Calisthenics, or bodyweight exercises, can be an excellent alternative to gym workouts. They build functional strength and muscle mass using your own body weight as resistance. And when it becomes too easy, you can switch to ring calisthenics or weighted calisthenics.

My favorite calisthenics exercises include:

- **Pull-ups**
- **Dips**
- **Muscle-ups**
- **Squats and pistol squats**
- **Lunges**
- **Australian pull ups**

I like to also do some push-ups with rings because there's some instability and you can add a rotation at the end of the movement to engage even more the chest.

Workout Frequency and Structure

Regardless of gender, when trying to gain weight, it's important not to overdo your workouts. Excessive exercise can increase calorie burn and create too much metabolic stress, making it harder to gain weight.

Recommended workout structure:

- Train 3-4 times per week maximum
- Choose one of the following split options:

1. 3 Full Body sessions per week
2. Push / Pull / Legs split
3. Push / Pull / Legs / Pull split

Sample 3 Full Body sessions per week:

- Monday: Full Body Workout A
- Wednesday: Full Body Workout B
- Friday: Full Body Workout C

Sample Push / Pull / Legs split:

- Monday: Push (chest, shoulders, triceps)
- Wednesday: Pull (back, biceps)
- Friday: Legs (quadriceps, hamstrings, calves)

Sample Push / Pull / Push / Pull split:

- Monday: Push
- Tuesday: Pull
- Thursday: Legs
- Friday: Pull

Remember to include rest days between workouts to allow for proper recovery and muscle growth. Adequate sleep and nutrition are crucial during this time. If you don't sleep well, then skip the next day's session and postpone it until the day after. This will prevent injury and help you perform better the next day.

For Women: Pilates or Resistance Training with Squats

For women looking to gain weight in a healthy way, focusing on exercises that build lean muscle mass and improve overall body composition is key. Two excellent options are Pilates and resistance training with a focus on squats.

Pilates is an excellent choice for women as it helps build core strength, improves posture, and develops lean muscle mass without excessive calorie burn.

Benefits of Pilates for weight gain:

- Builds strength and tones muscles without bulking
- Improves flexibility and posture
- Enhances mind-body connection
- Low-impact, reducing the risk of injury

A typical Pilates routine might include exercises like:

- The Hundred
- Roll-ups
- Leg circles
- Plank holds
- Side-lying leg lifts

If your goal is to build your best butt, then your best bet is to **go to the gym**. Incorporating resistance training, particularly squats, can be highly effective for women looking to gain weight. Squats are a compound exercise that engages multiple muscle groups, promoting overall muscle growth and strength.

Benefits of resistance training:

- Builds muscle mass in the lower body and core
- Increases overall strength
- Boosts metabolism, supporting healthy weight gain
- Improves bone density

A sample lower body resistance routine might include:

- Squats (3 sets of 8-12 reps)
- Lunges (3 sets of 10-15 reps per leg)
- Deadlifts (3 sets of 8-12 reps)
- Hip thrusts (3 sets of 12-15 reps)

Pre, Intra, and Post-Workout Nutrition

For pre-workout, ditch the weird pre-workout mixes and simply take a bit of baking soda (reduce lactic acid) or just some raw honey with salt.

Here's a quick and simple intra-workout beverage recipe:

- 500ml (about 16 oz) of filtered water
- Juice of 1/2 lemon
- 1 tablespoon of raw honey
- 1/4 teaspoon of high-quality sea salt or Himalayan pink salt

This beverage provides a balance of quick carbohydrates from honey, electrolytes from the salt, and a boost of vitamin C from the lemon. It can help maintain hydration, provide a small energy boost, and support electrolyte balance during your workout.

What you eat after your workout can significantly impact your body's ability to recover and build muscle. Here's a simple yet effective post-workout strategy:

After your workout, drink the juice of one or two freshly squeezed oranges with a good pinch of sea salt. This serves several purposes:

- Replenishes glycogen stores in the muscles
- Provides quick-absorbing carbohydrates to counteract

metabolic stress
- The salt helps replace electrolytes lost through sweat
- Vitamin C in oranges supports collagen production and immune function

Then, wait approximately 30 minutes or until hunger returns before consuming a full meal. This meal should be balanced and contain:

- High-quality protein
- Carbohydrates
- Healthy fats

One of the keys to successful weight gain is finding the right balance between exercise and nutrition. Your workout routine should stimulate muscle growth and increase appetite without creating excessive calorie burn. Combined with a calorie surplus from nutrient-dense foods, this approach will support healthy weight gain over time.

If you see that you're gaining too much fat, then you can incorporate one fast cardio session per week. In my case, I love skateboarding so I naturally do it to get around and it does my cardio and keeps my abs up.

Chapter 10 - Delicious Weight Gain Recipes

Welcome to the heart of your weight gain journey - the kitchen! This chapter is dedicated to providing you with a diverse array of calorie-dense, nutrient-rich recipes that will not only support your weight gain goals but also be super good for your gut.

From hearty stews that can be easily prepared in an Instant Pot or on the stovetop, to quick and delicious shakes for on-the-go nutrition, I've got you covered. I've also included some indulgent treats like homemade coconut ice cream (Ray Peat-inspired), because gaining weight should be also an enjoyable process!

You will see that many recipes are meat broths. They are delicious! The idea here is to extract the gelatin from the pieces of meat to benefit from their collagen and glycine. I do mine with the Instant Pot because it saves me so much more time than using a classic stovetop. But I've included here the recipes for both Instant Pot and stovetop. Each time you make these dishes, you can store the rich broth for use in cooking rice, for example.

Also, depending on whether you are gaining or losing weight, you can adapt the quantities and increase them if necessary.

Lamb Neck Stew with Potatoes

Lamb neck is a cheap cut but it's delicious. Lamb meat is known to be expensive but it's clearly not the case for lamb neck. It is cheaper than oxtail! And it is highly nutritious.

Ingredients:

- 8.8 oz lamb neck, cut into chunks
- 8.8 oz potatoes, peeled and cubed
- 1 onion, chopped
- 2 cloves garlic, minced
- 2 celery stalks, chopped
- 2 cups beef broth

- 1 tbsp olive oil
- Salt and pepper to taste

Instant Pot Instructions:

1. Set Instant Pot to Sauté mode. Add ghee and brown lamb chunks.
2. Add onion, garlic, and celery. Sauté for 2 minutes.
3. Add potatoes and broth. Close the lid and set High Pressure for 45 minutes.
4. Natural release for 10 minutes, then quick release.

Stovetop Instructions:

1. In a large pot, heat oil and brown lamb chunks.
2. Add onion, garlic, and celery. Sauté for 5 minutes.
3. Add potatoes and broth. Bring to a boil, then simmer for 3 hours until meat is tender.

Spaghetti alla Bolognese

I love Italian cuisine and this recipe is a basic. The grated cheese really makes all the difference. Go to an Italian grocery store for pecorino romano if you want even more flavor than parmesan.

Ingredients:

- 5.3 oz spaghetti
- 6.3 oz ground beef
- 5.3 oz tomato sauce
- 1 oz Parmigiano or Pecorino cheese, grated
- 1 small onion, finely chopped
- 2 cloves garlic, minced
- 1 tbsp olive oil
- Salt and pepper to taste

Instructions:

1. In a large pan, heat extra virgin olive oil over medium heat. Add onion and garlic, sauté until translucent.
2. Add ground beef, cook until browned.
3. Pour in tomato sauce, salt, and pepper. Simmer for 20 minutes.
4. Meanwhile, cook spaghetti according to package instructions.
5. Drain spaghetti, mix with the sauce, and top with grated cheese.

Oxtail with Celery and Rice

This recipe reminds me of the soups my grandmother used to make me in autumn and winter. It's very tasty and full of flavor. If you want to soften the taste of the beef, try using the cilantro.

Ingredients:

- 8.8 oz oxtail
- 6 0z rice
- 2 celery stalks, chopped
- 1 onion, chopped
- 2 cloves garlic, minced
- 2 cups beef broth
- 1 tbsp olive oil
- Salt and pepper to taste

Instant Pot Instructions:

1. Set Instant Pot to Sauté mode. Add ghee and brown oxtail pieces.
2. Add onion, garlic, and celery. Sauté for 2 minutes.
3. Add broth. Close lid and set to High Pressure for 45 minutes.
4. Natural release for 15 minutes, then quick release.

Stovetop Instructions:

1. In a large pot, heat ghee and brown oxtail pieces.
2. Add onion, garlic, and celery. Sauté for 5 minutes.
3. Add broth. Bring to a boil, then simmer for 2.5-3 hours until meat is tender.

Spaghetti with Mussels

I like this recipe because it allows you to eat shellfish, and frozen mussels are easy to find in supermarkets for those who don't live on the coast.

Ingredients:

- 5.3 oz spaghetti
- 7 oz mussels, cleaned
- 2 cloves garlic, minced
- 1/4 cup white wine
- 2 tbsp olive oil
- Chopped parsley
- Salt and pepper to taste

Instructions:

1. Cook spaghetti according to package instructions.
2. In a large pan, heat olive oil and sauté garlic.
3. Add mussels and white wine. Cover and cook until mussels open (about 5 minutes).
4. Toss cooked spaghetti with the mussel sauce, and garnish

with parsley.

Lamb or Veal Liver with Caramelized Onions and Honey

I eat liver 1 or 2 times a week because it's the most nutritious food in terms of vitamins. Before cooking, you can soak it in milk for 1 or 2 hours to soften its taste.

Ingredients:

- 7 oz lamb or veal liver, sliced
- 3.5 oz onions, sliced
- 2 tbsp honey
- 2 tbsp butter
- Salt and pepper to taste

Instructions:

1. Melt butter in a pan over medium heat. Add onions and cook until caramelized (about 15 minutes).
2. Push onions to the side, increase heat, and add liver slices.
3. Cook liver for 2-3 minutes each side.
4. Add honey, stir to combine with onions and liver. Cook for another minute.

Oven-Baked Cheesy Potatoes

These potatoes are very easy to make if you have an oven, and adding a slice of melting cheese at the end makes all the difference.

CHAPTER 10 - DELICIOUS WEIGHT GAIN RECIPES

Ingredients:

- 8.8 oz potatoes sliced
- 2 oz cheese (I use camembert because it has a strong cheese taste)
- 1/4 cup heavy cream
- 1 clove garlic, minced
- Salt and pepper to taste

Instructions:

1. Preheat oven to 375°F (190°C).
2. Layer potato slices in a baking dish. Sprinkle with garlic, salt, and pepper.
3. Bake for 45-50 minutes until potatoes are tender.
4. Top the potatoes with Camembert slices over each slide of potatoes and let it melt.

Ray Peat Carrot Salad

Ray Peat's carrot salad should be eaten between meals to lower the level of endotoxins in your gut.

Ingredients:

- 1 large carrot, grated
- 1 tbsp coconut oil, melted or not
- 1 tsp apple cider vinegar
- Pinch of salt

Instructions:

1. Grate the carrot lengthwise to preserve the long fibers (the fibers will swipe endotoxins in your gut).
2. Mix with melted coconut oil, apple cider vinegar, and salt.

Homemade Coconut Ice Cream

I found this recipe on recipeats.org and being a coconut fan I love this ice cream. This method creates a rich, creamy ice cream without the need for an ice cream maker. The frequent stirring helps create a smooth texture. For best results, consume within a week of making.

Ingredients:

- 1 large egg + 1 yolk (pastured, room temperature)

- 1 cup pure cane sugar
- 1 cup coconut oil
- 2 cups milk
- Optional: 1 tsp vanilla extract, pinch of pickling salt
- Optional: Coffee or fruit for flavoring

Instructions:

1. In a mixing bowl, combine the sugar, whole egg, and egg yolk. Blend on low speed until well mixed.
2. Heat the coconut oil to 95°F (40°C).
3. Slowly pour the heated coconut oil into the sugar and egg mixture while blending on low speed.
4. Heat the milk to 95°F (40°C).
5. Gradually add the warm milk to the mixture, continuing to blend on low speed.
6. If desired, add optional flavorings such as vanilla extract, a pinch of pickling salt, coffee, or fruit.
7. Pour the mixture into a covered container.
8. Place the container in the freezer. Every 3-4 hours, remove and mix or churn the mixture to prevent large ice crystals from forming.
9. The ice cream is ready when it's fully frozen, which typically takes about 6-8 hours or overnight.

High-Calorie Milkshake

I sometimes use this milkshake when I want to make something quick because there's not even any need for a blender!

Ingredients:

- 1 egg
- 3.2 oz raw milk
- 1.9 oz raw cream
- 2 tbsp honey

Instructions: Blend or shake all ingredients until smooth. Consume immediately.

Papaya Cream

Papaya cream is an original dessert that's excellent for soothing the stomach.

Ingredients:

- 1 egg
- 1 oz (30g) raw butter
- 5.3 oz (150g) ripe papaya, peeled and seeded
- 0.7 oz (20g) honey

Instructions:

1. In a blender or food processor, combine the egg, papaya, and honey. Blend until smooth.
2. Melt the raw butter using a double boiler method (bain-marie).
3. Add the melted butter to the papaya mixture in the blender.
4. Blend everything together until well combined and creamy.
5. The papaya cream is now ready to serve. You can chill it before serving if you prefer a cooler dessert.

Apple Sauce

Making large quantities of applesauce is a great way to have a good-quality dessert always ready in the fridge! If you have trouble digesting fruit, apples are more easily assimilated when cooked.

CHAPTER 10 - DELICIOUS WEIGHT GAIN RECIPES

Ingredients:

- 8 apples, peeled, cored, and chopped
- 2 tbsp butter
- 2 tbsp honey
- 1 tsp cinnamon
- 1/4 cup water

Instructions:

1. In a saucepan, combine all ingredients.
2. Bring to a boil, then reduce heat and simmer for 15-20

minutes until apples are soft.
3. Mash with a fork for a chunky sauce, or blend for smooth sauce.

Instant Pot Instructions:

1. Place all ingredients in the Instant Pot.
2. Close the lid and set the valve to sealing position.
3. Cook on High Pressure for 3 minutes.
4. Once the cooking time is complete, allow for a Natural Pressure Release for 15 minutes, then carefully do a Quick Release for any remaining pressure.
5. Open the lid and mash the apples or use an immersion blender for a smooth sauce.
6. If the sauce is too watery, use the Sauté function to simmer and reduce the liquid, stirring frequently.

Chapter 11 - Tips for Staying Motivated

Gaining weight when you're naturally thin with a fast metabolism can be difficult. There are many factors to consider and a diet to improve. Nevertheless, little by little, you can integrate the concepts described in this book to gain weight healthily. Here are some tips that will help you stay motivated, but also keep track of your progress. I'll remind you: It's a marathon, not a sprint.

Set Realistic Goals: Understanding your starting point and setting achievable milestones

Setting realistic goals is crucial for maintaining motivation and avoiding disappointment. Start by assessing your current situation and determine your daily calorie intake.

Once you have a target, break it down into short-term and long-term goals. **A healthy rate of weight gain is typically 0.5-1 lb (0.2-0.4 kg) per week.** Set 3-month, 6-month, and

1-year targets based on this rate.

Create action-based goals to support your weight gain: daily calorie intake targets, weekly workout plans, and meal preparation schedules if you have a really busy life… By focusing on actions you can control, rather than just the result, you'll find it easier to stay motivated and on track.

Track Food and Weight Gain, But Don't Obsess: Importance of staying on track without creating unhealthy habits

Tracking your food intake and weight can be helpful, but it's important to maintain a healthy relationship with these metrics. Consider using a food tracking app like Cronometer for the first few weeks to understand your calorie intake. This can be eye-opening and help you identify areas where you can increase your calories healthfully.

For weight tracking, aim for weekly weigh-ins at the same time of day. **Don't do it every day because your weight will fluctuate a lot due to factors like water retention and digestion**, so don't be discouraged by small day-to-day changes. Focus on the overall trend over time.

While tracking can be useful, it's crucial to avoid obsessive behaviors. If you find yourself feeling anxious about tracking every morsel, it might be time to step back and consider a more intuitive eating approach. The goal is to nourish your body, not to create stress around food and weight.

Recognizing non-scale victories such as increased energy, better mood, and improved digestion

Weight gain is just one measure of progress. Pay attention to increases in energy levels, improvements in mood, and better digestion. You might notice enhanced physical performance, better sleep quality, or improvements in your skin, hair, and nail health.

Keep a journal to record these improvements. On days when motivation is low, reviewing these small wins can reignite your commitment to your goals. Key indicators to monitor include energy levels, libido, mood, and digestion. **Keep a daily log rating your energy from 1-10, note any changes in libido or sexual performance, and track your emotional state and digestive health**.

In terms of digestion, pay attention to bowel movement frequency and quality. These indicators provide a comprehensive view of how your weight gain journey is impacting your overall health and well-being.

Take progress photos and regular weigh-ins to track physical changes

Visual photos can also provide concrete evidence of your progress. Take progress photos every weeks, ensuring consistent clothing, lighting, and positioning. Photograph yourself from the front, side, and back for a complete view. Move all those photos to the same folder so you can quickly see the differences and the progression. Remember, progress isn't always linear. There may be weeks where you don't see changes, and that's okay. The key is to look at the overall trend over time.

Stay patient, stay consistent, and **trust the process**. Your dedication will pay off, resulting in not just weight gain, but improved overall health and quality of life.

Chapter 12 - How to Increase Calories Without Changing Everyone's Menu

Gaining weight when you don't have full control over your meals can be extremely difficult. Many people find themselves in situations where they live with family members or partners who have different dietary habits or preferences. This common struggle often leaves those trying to gain weight feeling stuck between their personal goals and the desire to maintain household harmony.

The challenge lies in finding ways to increase calorie intake without disrupting established meal routines or causing inconvenience to others. It's a delicate balance – you want to respect the dietary habits of those you live with while still meeting your nutritional needs. Let's explore practical strategies to boost your calorie intake subtly and effectively, without the need for drastic changes to family meals.

Strategies to Boost Calorie Intake Without Complicating Family Meals

Add-on Foods

One of the simplest ways to increase your calorie intake is by adding calorie-dense foods to your existing meals. These additions can be seamless and won't affect the overall dish for others. Some examples include:

- Drizzling extra virgin olive oil or butter over your rice, pasta, potatoes...
- Sprinkling cheese on top of your meals where appropriate
- Take one tbsp of honey at the end of the dish, or take it with an infusion
- Explain your goals and take bigger portions than usual. Be mindful of others, ensuring there's enough for everyone, but don't be shy about going for seconds if they're available.

These small additions can slightly increase your calorie intake without altering the core meal for others.

Introduce a 4 PM Snack and control your breakfast

If your family doesn't typically have an afternoon snack, introducing one for yourself can be an excellent way to boost your calorie intake. This snack time is usually when you're alone or not interfering with family meal times.

I've shared with you my favorite 4 PM snack in Chapter 10: **Papaya cream, High-calorie milkshake, Cheese with dried figs or dates and honey, Cooked apple with butter and goat cheese...**

Breakfast is often consumed alone, making it a perfect opportunity to take full control of your calorie intake. Use these meals to really pack in the nutrients and calories.

Drink Raw Goat Milk Between Meals

Introducing **raw goat milk as a between-meal drink can be a game-changer for weight gain**. It's nutrient-dense and calorie-rich, making it an excellent choice for those looking to increase their intake. Treat it like you would water, sipping it throughout the day.

Cook for Your Family

Taking the initiative to cook for your family can be a win-win situation. By volunteering to prepare meals once or twice a week, you gain control over the menu while also contributing to the household. This is your chance to introduce nutrient-dense, calorie-rich meals that support your weight gain goals while still being enjoyable for everyone.

Dishes like lamb neck stew or spaghetti alla Bolognese are perfect examples. They're easy to prepare in large quantities and great for weight gain. To get your family on board, you can highlight the benefits: **mention to your mother and sisters that the broth is excellent for collagen production and skin** (less acne, wrinkles, better tone…), and tell your father and brothers it's the kind of real, wholesome food your ancestors thrived on.

Another excellent approach is to recreate family favorites. If there's a dish your grandmother is famous for, ask for the recipe and try to master it. Often, traditional family recipes are naturally more suitable for weight gain and gut health than modern alternatives. For instance, learning to make authentic spaghetti alla carbonara (using guanciale instead of bacon) can be a great way to incorporate a fatty, calorie-dense meal that your family will appreciate.

If you're new to cooking, start with simple recipes. The coconut ice cream and oven-baked cheesy potatoes with ground meat mentioned earlier in the book are great options for beginners. These dishes are straightforward to prepare and can easily feed a family.

Remember, the key is to stay flexible and adaptable. While you're focusing on your weight gain goals, it's important to consider your family's preferences. By taking this approach, you're not just working towards your personal goals, but also contributing positively to family meal times.

Implementing these strategies allows you to increase your calorie intake subtly yet effectively without disrupting your family's established eating habits. It's about making small, consistent changes that add up over time. These strategies will help you make progress without causing friction at home. Stay patient, be creative with your additions and cooking, and you'll find that reaching your weight gain goals while living with others can be achievable.

Conclusion

You now have all the knowledge you need to gain weight. Even if you are naturally thin with a very fast metabolism. But you won't fall into the same error patterns that I fell into myself! I wish I were in your place, at the beginning of my weight gain journey, because at that time there were no books on the subject and it was very experimental.

It took me years to gain weight, even just 11 or 22 lbs. But by applying the advice I've shared with you in the book, I really saw the difference in my weight. And quickly. I assure you that you will gain weight if you apply just 50% of the advice I give in the book. Certainly, it won't be easy, but a few months of perseverance will show you that it's possible and that you are gaining weight.

Read this book several times and take notes to really master this volume of information.

Wishing you successful weight gain,
   -**Pierre Tom.**

Resources

n the resources web page, you will find:

- Links of supplements mentioned in the chapter 8,
- Cookware I use,
- Vagus nerve reset tutorial,
- Light friendly bulbs and glasses,
- Websites and apps mentioned.

Unlock those resources by scanning this QR code:

Quick guide to scanning:

1. Launch your phone's camera app
2. Aim it at the QR code above
3. Tap the pop-up link

No luck? Make sure QR scanning is enabled in your camera settings, or grab a free QR scanner app from your app store.

Printed in Dunstable, United Kingdom